PRAY THE WORD

JOY HANEY

PRAY THE WORD

JOY HANEY

PRAY THE WORD
by Joy Haney

2nd Printing, 2004

All Scripture quotations in this booklet are from the King James Version of the Bible unless otherwise identified.

ISBN #1-880969-49-1

Printed in the United States of America

CONTENTS

Foreword

TO FIGHT IS ESSENTIAL

Nehemiah 4:14 declares: "Be not ye afraid of them: remember the LORD, which is great and terrible, and FIGHT for your brethren, your sons, and your daughters, your wives, and your houses."

The Spirit is saying today: FIGHT FOR YOUR SONS AND DAUGHTERS AND YOUR HOUSEHOLDS—THIS MEANING THE FAMILY HOUSEHOLD AND THE HOUSEHOLD OF FAITH—OUR HERITAGE

Life itself is a fight. We begin to fight the minute we are born. A baby comes out fighting and gasping for life. When that first breath comes, the first fight is won.

It is established in the Scriptures that the Lord will teach us to fight. It is stated in Psalm 144:1-2: "Blessed be the LORD my strength, which teacheth my hands to war, and my fingers to fight: My goodness, and my fortress; my high tower, and my deliver; my shield, and he in whom I trust; who subdueth my people under me."

Paul, the apostle, said that he was in a fight for his life. I Corinthians 9:26 refers to this fight: "I therefore so run, not as uncertainly; so fight I, not as one that beateth the air." He shares the key to winning the fight in verse 27: "But I keep under my body, and bring it into subjection."

Today we must fight against the devil, the flesh, the world, evil spirits, evil thoughts, and the onslaught of the enemy. The *enemy* is anything that would keep us, our families, our churches, and others from being saved, and living an abundant life in Christ Jesus.

ADVERSITY IS NOT OPTIONAL!

Jesus Himself said in John 16:33: "In the world ye shall have tribulation." But in the same breath, He said, "But be of good cheer; I have overcome the world."

We will not fight in the flesh, but in the Spirit. When Jesus and the disciples were in the Garden of Gethsemane, Peter fought in the flesh. He pulled out a sword and cut off the enemy's ear and while blood spurted, Jesus just picked the ear up and placed it back on the man's head and said, "Put your sword up."

Jesus told Pilate: "My kingdom is not of this world: if my kingdom were of this world, then would my servants fight, that I should not be delivered to the Jews: but now is my kingdom not from hence."

We do not fight this with actual swords, but with the Sword of the Spirit. Paul declares this to be so in Ephesians 6:12: "For we wrestle not against flesh and blood, but against principalities, against powers, against the rulers of the darkness of this world, against spiritual wickedness in high places."

We will not just waltz into heaven, but we will fight our way there. It will be bloody, tough, and at times almost unbearable, but we must remember WHO is on our side. This is emphasized in Romans 8:31:

"What shall we then say to these things? If God be for us, who can be against us?"

In the Old Testament when Sennacherib came against King Hezekiah and threatened to destroy him, Hezekiah rent his clothes and went into the house of the Lord.

He was going to battle in the Spirit realm. He called on God and asked for help. God said, "Be not afraid, I will defend the city." The end result was that God sent ONE angel to fight against the Assyrian army, and when they were supposed to get up in the morning, they remained lying in their cots because they couldn't move. You see in the nighttime, God sent an angel, and there were 185,000 dead corpses (II Kings 19:35).

God does wonderful things in the nighttimes of our lives. That is when the supernatural power begins to work. When we have lost control, when we have no more strength, not sure what to do, we call on God, and He comes in the nighttimes and performs a miracle.

In Judges 6, there is a story told of Gideon. The angel of the Lord appeared to Gideon and told him, "The LORD is with thee, thou mighty man of valour."

Notice how Gideon answered him, "Oh my LORD, if the LORD be with us, why then is all this befallen us? and where be all his miracles which our fathers told us of, saying, Did not the LORD bring us up from Egypt? but now the LORD hath forsaken us, and delivered us into the hands of the Midianites" (Judges 6:13).

Is that not like the way we are? We say in so many words: "If you're with us, why hast this happened to us? I hear everyone around me talking of miracles and deliverances while I'm still waiting for you to answer."

God answered Gideon in Judges 6: 14: "And the LORD looked upon him, and said, Go in this thy might, and thou shalt save Israel from the hand of the Midianites: have not I sent thee?"

Gideon still argued with him. He said, "Oh, my LORD, wherewith shall I save Israel? behold, my family is poor in Manasseh, and I am the least in my father's house" (Judges 6:15).

We look at ourselves differently than God does. He sees what we can do with Him fighting with us!

Verse 16: "And the LORD said unto him, Surely I will be with thee, and thou shalt smite the Midianites as one man."

Verse 33: "Then all the Midianites and the Amalekites and the children of the east were gathered together and went over, and pitched in the valley of Jezreel." They were setting up for the kill.

But watch what happened in verse 34: "But the Spirit of the Lord came upon Gideon, and he blew a trumpet." This was a call for war! 32,000 men came, but God said there were "too many" men. He told Gideon to tell those who were fearful and afraid to go home. There were 22,000 who went home.

There remained 10,000 men, but God said, there are still "too many" men. So He gave them the water test and only 300 passed the test.

God said, "You take these 300 men, divide them into 3 companies and spread them out around the camp of the Midianites."

Here it was again: It was in the nighttime. God told Gideon to give each man a trumpet. They were to hold it in one hand, and in the other hand, they were to hold a pitcher with a lamp inside.

Gideon said, "When I blow my trumpet, then every man is to blow his trumpet and cry "The SWORD OF THE LORD AND OF GIDEON." Then break the pitcher and let the light shine.

Is not this still God's way, to "Blow the trumpet and let the light shine?"

This speaks to me of the power of the Word and of prayer. In one hand, they had a trumpet, and the other hand, they had a light. Does not the Bible say "Thy word is a lamp unto my feet, and a light unto my path" (Psalm 119:105)? And did not Isaiah 58:1 say, "Cry aloud, spare not, lift up thy voice like a trumpet"?

What was the voice crying? It was crying forth the Word of the Lord.

Then they were to cry, "The sword of the LORD and of Gideon." God's sword and Gideon's sword working together fighting against the enemy: it was an unbeatable combination.

It is the same today: we have God's Spirit working in our behalf, "Not by might, nor by power, but by my Spirit, saith the LORD." And we have our sword, which is the Word of God spoken of in Ephesians 6:17: "And take the helmet of salvation, and the sword of the Spirit, which is the word of God." Verse 18: "Praying always with all prayer and supplication in the Spirit."

God's ways are unorthodox. You do not have to be smart to win, you just have to be surrendered and obey the Lord. It is not what you think about yourself—it is what God thinks about you.

God has given us a sword to fight with. It is

described in Hebrews 4:12: "For the word of God is quick, and powerful, and sharper than any twoedged sword, piercing even to the dividing asunder of soul and spirit, and of the joints and marrow, and is a discerner of the thoughts and intents of the heart."

We must fight with the Word, with prayer, and in the name of Jesus as spoken of in Psalm 20:7: "Some trust in chariots, and some in horses: but we will remember the name of the LORD our God."

E.M. Bounds said, "Prayer is of transcendent importance. Prayer is the mightiest agent to advance God's work. Prayer succeeds when all else fails."

This booklet will help you use one of the best ways to fight against evil, sickness, disease, trouble, or anything that brings distress of mind. It is to PRAY THE WORD. God's Word is very powerful and nothing can stand in its way, as stated in the following scriptures:

Isaiah 40:8:

The grass withereth, the flower fadeth: but the word of our God shall stand for ever.

Psalm 12:6-7:

Verses:

6. The words of the LORD are pure words: as silver tried in a furnace of earth, purified seven times.
7. Thou shalt keep them, O LORD, thou shalt preserve them from this generation for ever.

God is God and there is none beside Him!

Isaiah 45: 5-6:

Verses:

5. I am the LORD, and there is none else, there is

no God beside me: I girded thee, though thou hast not known me:

6. That they may know from the rising of the sun, and from the west, that there is none beside me. I am the LORD, and there is none else.

Isaiah 55:11:
So shall my word be that goeth forth out of my mouth: it shall not return unto me void, but it shall accomplish that which I please, and it shall prosper in the thing whereto I sent it.

Hebrews 11:3:
Through faith we understand that the worlds were framed by the word of God, so that things which are seen were not made of things which do appear.

Jeremiah 33:14:
Behold, the days come, saith the LORD, that I will perform that good thing which I have promised.

The Word of God is so powerful that it keeps the sea from overflowing its borders.
Jeremiah 5:22:
Fear ye not me? saith the LORD: will ye not tremble at my presence, which have placed the sand for the bound of the sea by a perpetual decree, that it cannot pass it: and though the waves thereof toss themselves, yet can they not prevail; though they roar, yet can they not pass over it?

Psalm 138:2:
I will worship toward thy holy temple, and praise thy

name for thy lovingkindness and for thy truth: for thou hast magnified thy word above all thy name.

Pray the Word . . .

When Attacked by People or the Enemy

Psalm 35:

Verses:

1. Plead my cause, O Lord, with them that strive with me: fight against them that fight against me.
2. Take hold of shield and buckler, and stand up for mine help.
3. Draw out also the spear, and stop the way against them that persecute me: say unto my soul, I am thy salvation.
4. Let them be confounded and put to shame that seek after my soul: let them be turned back and brought to confusion that devise my hurt.
5. Let them be as chaff before the wind: and let the angel of the Lord chase them.
6. Let their way be dark and slippery: and let the angel of the Lord persecute them.
7. For without cause have they hid for me their net in a pit, which without cause they have digged for my soul.
8. Let destruction come upon him at unawares; and let his net he hath hid catch himself: into that very destruction let him fall.
9. And my soul shall be joyful in the Lord: it shall rejoice in his salvation.
10. All my bones shall say, Lord, who is like unto thee, which deliverest the poor from him that is too strong for him, yea, the poor and the needy from him that spoileth him?
11. False witnesses did rise up; they laid to my charge things that I knew not.
12. They rewarded me evil for good to the spoiling of my soul.

13. But as for me, when they were sick, my clothing was sackcloth: I humbled my soul with fasting; and my prayer returned into mine own bosom.
14. I behaved myself as though he had been my friend or brother: I bowed down heavily, as one that mourneth for his mother.
15. But in mine adversity they rejoiced, and gathered themselves together; yea, the abjects gathered themselves together against me, and I knew it not; they did tear me, and ceased not;
16. With hypocritical mockers in feasts, they gnashed upon me with their teeth.
17. Lord, how long wilt thou look on? Rescue my soul from their destructions, my darling from the lions.
18. I will give thee thanks in the great congregation: I will praise thee among much people.
19. Let not them that are mine enemies wrongfully rejoice over me: neither let them wink with the eye that hate me without a cause.
20. For they speak not peace: but they devise deceitful matters against them that are quiet in the land.
21. Yea, they opened their mouth wide against me, and said, Aha, aha, our eye hath seen it.
22. This thou hast seen, O Lord: keep not silence: O Lord, be not far from me.
23. Stir up thyself, and awake to my judgment, even unto my cause, my God and my Lord.
24. Judge me, O Lord my God, according to thy righteousness; and let them not rejoice over me.
25. Let them not say in their hearts, Ah, so would we have it: let them not say, We have swallowed

him up.

26. Let them be ashamed and brought to confusion together that rejoice at mine hurt: let them be clothed with shame and dishonour that magnify themselves against me.
27. Let them shout for joy, and be glad, that favour my righteous cause: yea, let them say continually, Let the LORD be magnified, which hath pleasure in the prosperity of his servant.
28. And my tongue shall speak of thy righteousness and of thy praise all the day long.

Psalm 64:

Verses:

1. Hear my voice, O God, in my prayer: preserve my life from fear of the enemy.
2. Hide me from the secret counsel of the wicked; from the insurrection of the workers of iniquity:
3. Who whet their tongue like a sword, and bend their bows to shoot their arrows, even bitter words:
4. That they may shoot in secret at the perfect: suddenly do they shoot at him, and fear not.
5. They encourage themselves in an evil matter: they commune of laying snares privily; they say, Who shall see them?
6. They search out iniquities; they accomplish a diligent search: both the inward thought of every one of them, and the heart, is deep.
7. But God shall shoot at them with an arrow; suddenly shall they be wounded.
8. So they shall make their own tongue to fall upon themselves: all that see them shall flee

away.

9. And all men shall fear, and shall declare the word of God; for they shall wisely consider of his doing.
10. The righteous shall be glad in the LORD, and shall trust in him; and all the upright in heart shall glory.

Psalm 140:

Verses:

1. Deliver me, O LORD, from the evil man;
2. Which imagine mischiefs in their heart; continually are they gathered together for war.
3. They have sharpened their tongues like a serpent; adders' poison is under their lips. Selah.
4. Keep me, O LORD, from the hands of the wicked; preserve me from the violent man; who have purposed to overthrow my goings.
5. The proud have hid a snare for me, and cords; they have spread a net by the wayside; they have set gins for me. Selah.
6. I said unto the LORD, Thou art my God: hear the voice of my supplications, O LORD.
7. O God the LORD, the strength of my salvation, thou hast covered my head in the day of battle.
8. Grant not, O LORD, the desires of the wicked: further not his wicked device; lest they exalt themselves. Selah.
9. As for the head of those that compass me about, let the mischief of their own lips cover them.
10. Let burning coals fall upon them: let them be cast into the fire; into deep pits, that they rise

not up again.

11. Let not an evil speaker be established in the earth: evil shall hunt the violent man to overthrow him.
12. I know that the LORD will maintain the cause of the afflicted, and the right of the poor.
13. Surely the righteous shall give thanks unto thy name: the upright shall dwell in thy presence.

Psalm 18:47-48:

Verses:

47. It is God that avengeth me, and subdueth the people under me.
48. He delivereth me from mine enemies: yea, thou liftest me up above those that rise up against me: thou hast delivered me from the violent man.

Psalm 18:2-3:

Verses:

2. The LORD is my rock, and my fortress, and my deliverer; my God, my strength, in whom I will trust; my buckler, and the horn of my salvation, and my high tower.
3. I will call upon the LORD, who is worthy to be praised: so shall I be saved from mine enemies.

Isaiah 54:17:

No weapon that is formed against thee shall prosper; and every tongue that shall rise against thee in judgment thou shalt condemn. This is the heritage of the servants of the LORD, and their righteousness is of me, saith the LORD.

PRAY THE WORD . . .

Over Your Family

NOTE: In some of the following scriptures, the singular nouns and pronouns have been changed to make the prayers applicable for the family because a family is more than one person.

Psalm 17:8:

Keep our family as the apple of the eye, hide us under the shadow of thy wings.

Psalm 20:5-8:

Verses:

5. We will rejoice in thy salvation, and in the name of our God we will set up our banners: the LORD fulfil all our petitions.
6. Now know we that the LORD saveth his anointed; he will hear him from his holy heaven with the saving strength of his right hand.
7. Some trust in chariots, and some in horses: but we will remember the name of the LORD our God.
8. They are brought down and fallen: be we are risen, and stand upright.

Psalm 27:1:

The LORD is our light and our salvation; whom shall we fear? the LORD is the strength of our life; of whom shall we be afraid?

Psalm 28:7:

The LORD is our strength and our shield; our hearts trusted in him, and we are helped: therefore our hearts greatly rejoiceth; and with our song will we praise him.

Psalm 29:11:

The LORD will give strength unto our family; the LORD will bless our family with peace.

Psalm 32:7 & 8:

Verses:

7. Thou art our hiding place; thou shalt preserve our family from trouble; thou shalt compass us about with songs of deliverance. Selah.
8. You will instruct us and teach us in the way which we should go: You will guide us with your eye.

Psalm 33:20-22:

Verses:

20. Our soul waiteth for the LORD: he is our help and our shield
21. For our heart shall rejoice in him, because we have trusted in his holy name.
22. Let thy mercy, O LORD, be upon us, according as we hope in thee.

Psalm 56:3-4:

Verses:

3. What time we are afraid, we will trust in thee.
4. In God we will praise his word, in God we have put our trust; we will not fear what flesh can do unto us.

Psalm 67:1:

God be merciful unto us, and bless us; and cause his face to shine upon us; Selah.

Psalm 71:1-3:

Verses:

1. In thee, O LORD, do we put our trust: let us never be put to confusion.
2. Deliver us in thy righteousness, and cause us to escape: incline thine ear unto us, and save us.
3. Be thou our strong habitation, whereunto we may continually resort: thou hast given commandment to save us; for thou art our rock and our fortress.

Psalm 90:12, 14, & 17:

Verses:

12. Teach us to number our days, that we may apply our hearts unto wisdom.
14. O satisfy us early with thy mercy; that we may rejoice and be glad all our days.
17. And let the beauty of the LORD our God be upon us: and establish thou the work of our hands upon us: yea, the work of our hands establish thou it.

Lord, plant our family in Your house as described in the Psalm.

Psalm 92: 13-14:

Verses:

13. Those that be planted in the house of the LORD shall flourish in the courts of our God.
14. They shall still bring forth fruit in old age; they shall be fat and flourishing.

Psalm 106:4:
Remember us, O LORD, with the favour that thou bearest unto thy people: O visit us with thy salvation.

Psalm 119:133-135:
Verses:
133. Order our steps in thy word: and let not any iniquity have dominion over us.
134. Deliver us from the oppression of man: so will we keep thy precepts.
135. Make thy face to shine upon thy servants, and teach us thy statutes.

Psalm 121:7-8:
Verses:
7. LORD, preserve us from all evil: preserve our soul.
8. LORD, preserve our going out and coming in from this time forth, and even for evermore.

Psalm 143: 8, 10-11:
Verses:
8. Cause us to hear thy lovingkindness in the morning; for in thee do we trust: cause us to know the way wherein we should walk; for we lift up our souls unto thee.
10. Teach us to do thy will; for thou art our God: thy spirit is good; lead us into the land of uprightness.
11. Quicken us, O LORD, for thy name's sake: for thy righteousness' sake bring our soul out of trouble.

Help our family, Lord, to make the right choices and to love You dearly, so Your blessing will be upon us as stated in,

Deuteronomy 30:19-20:

Verses:

19. I have set before you life and death, blessing and cursing: therefore choose life, that both thou and thy seed may live:
20. That thou mayest love the LORD thy God, and that thou mayest obey his voice, and that thou mayest cleave unto him: for he is thy life, and the length of thy days.

I Chronicles 4:10:

And Jabez called on the God of Israel, saying, Oh that thou wouldest bless me indeed, and enlarge my coast, and that thine hand might be with me, and that thou wouldest keep me from evil, that it may not grieve me! And God granted him that which he requested.

O God, bless our family indeed. Enlarge our coast and influence so that You will be glorified through us. Keep Your hand upon us and keep us from evil so it will not bring grief to our family. In Jesus' name!

Lord, as Caleb asked for a mountain and his daughter asked for a blessing, we are asking for challenges and the strength to accomplish them. We are asking for blessings and plentiful springs in our lives.

Joshua 14:12:

Give me this mountain, whereof the LORD spake in that day.

Joshua 15:19:

Give me a blessing; for thou hast given me a south land; give me also springs of water. And he gave her the upper springs, and the nether springs.

Pray the Word . . .

When There Is Sickness

Isaiah 53:5:

But he was wounded for our transgressions, he was bruised for our iniquities: the chastisement of our peace was upon him; and with his stripes we are healed.

I Peter 2:24:

Who his own self bare our sins in his own body on the tree, that we, being dead to sins, should live unto righteousness: by whose stripes ye were healed.

Exodus 15:26:

If thou wilt diligently hearken to the voice of the Lord thy God, and wilt do that which is right in his sight, and wilt give ear to his commandments, and keep all his statutes, I will put none of these diseases upon thee, which have brought upon the Egyptians: for I am the Lord God that healeth thee.

Psalm 107:19-20:

Verses:

19. Then they cry unto the Lord in their trouble, and he saveth them out of their distresses.
20. He sent his Word, and healed them, and delivered them from their destructions.

III John 2:

Beloved, I wish above all thing that thou mayest prosper and be in health, even as thy soul prospereth.

Mark 5:36:

Lord, I accept the words You spoke to the ruler of

the synagogue in behalf of his daughter's sickness and even death.

Jesus said to him: "Be not afraid, only believe."

I believe in Jesus' name for my healing!

Psalm 118:17:

I shall not die, but live, and declare the works of the LORD.

Psalm 33:18-20:

Verses:

18. Behold, the eye of the LORD is upon them that fear him, upon them that hope in his mercy;
19. To deliver their soul from death, and to keep them alive in famine.
20. Our soul waiteth for the LORD: he is our help and our shield.

Psalm 30:2-3:

Verses:

2. O LORD my God, I cried unto thee, and thou hast healed me.
3. O LORD, thou hast brought up my soul from the grave: thou hast kept me alive, that I should not go down to the pit.

Lord, Your Word says in III John 2 that it is Your will for me to have health. I Peter 2:24 states, by Your stripes we were healed. I accept that healing today and stand on Your Word. Teach me the ways of health, and give me optimum health. You said, "I am the Lord God that healeth thee."

Lord, I shine Your laser Word into the central part

of my sickness and disease. Cut it out—make it disappear—as Your Word says, "He sent his Word and healed them." I stand on the Word today in faith believing.

Pray the Word . . .

Over a Broken Heart

Psalm 147:3:
He healeth the broken in heart, and bindeth up their wounds.

Heal my broken heart, and bind up my wounds.

Psalm 119:28:
My soul melteth for heaviness: strengthen thou me according unto thy word.

Psalm 107:28-29:
Verses:
28. Then they cry unto the LORD in their trouble, and he bringeth them out of their distresses.
29. He maketh the storm a calm, so that the waves thereof are still.

Psalm 34:17-19:
Verses:
17. The righteous cry, and the LORD heareth, and delivereth them out of all their troubles.
18. The LORD is nigh unto them that are of a broken heart; and saveth such as be of a contrite spirit.
19. Many are the afflictions of the righteous: but the LORD delivereth him out of them all.

The Lord is nigh unto me, and He is going to deliver me from this heartbreaking situation.

Psalm 69:20, 29-33:
Verses:
20. Reproach hath broken my heart; and I am full of heaviness: and I looked for some to take pity,

but there was none; and for comforters, but I found none.

29. But I am poor and sorrowful: let thy salvation, O God, set me up on high.
30. I will praise the name of God with a song, and will magnify him with thanksgiving.
31. This also shall please the LORD better than an ox or bullock that hath horns and hoofs.
32. The humble shall see this, and be glad: and your heart shall live that seek God.
33. For the LORD heareth the poor, and despiseth not his prisoners.

Isaiah 61:1:

The Spirit of the LORD God is upon me; because the LORD hath anointed me to preach good tidings unto the meek; he hath sent me to bind up the broken-hearted, to proclaim liberty to the captives, and the opening of the prison to them that are bound.

Luke 4:18:

The Spirit of the Lord is upon me, because he hath anointed me to preach the gospel to the poor; he hath sent me to heal the brokenhearted, to preach deliverance to the captives, and recovering of sight to the blind, to set at liberty them that are bruised.

Psalm 40:11-13 & 17:

Verses:

11. Withhold not thou thy tender mercies from me, O LORD: let thy lovingkindness and thy truth continually preserve me.
12. For innumerable evils have compassed me about:

mine iniquities have taken hold upon me, so that I am not able to look up; they are more than the hairs of mine head: therefore my heart faileth me.

13. Be pleased, O LORD, to deliver me: O LORD, make haste to help me.
17. But I am poor and needy; yet the LORD thinketh upon me: thou art my help and my deliverer; make no tarrying, O my God.

Psalm 9:9-10:

Verses:

9. The LORD also will be a refuge for the oppressed, a refuge in times of trouble.
10. And they that know thy name will put their trust in thee: for thou, LORD, hast not forsaken them that seek thee.

Psalm 61:1-3:

Verses:

1. Hear my cry, O God; attend unto my prayer.
2. From the end of the earth will I cry unto thee, when my heart is overwhelmed: lead me to the rock that is higher than I.
3. For thou hast been a shelter for me, and a strong tower from the enemy.

Lamentations 3:19-26:

Verses:

19. Remembering mine affliction and my misery, the wormwood and the gall.
20. My soul hath them still in remembrance, and is humbled in me.
21. This I recall to my mind, therefore have I hope.

22. It is of the Lord's mercies that we are not consumed, because his compassions fail not.
23. They are new every morning: great is thy faithfulness.
24. The Lord is my portion, saith my soul; therefore will I hope in him.
25. The Lord is good unto them that wait for him, to the soul that seeketh him.
26. It is good that a man should both hope and quietly wait for the salvation of the Lord.

Pray the Word . . .

In Times of Fear

Psalm 34:4-10:

Verses:

4. I sought the LORD, and he heard me, and delivered me from all my fears.
5. They looked unto him, and were lightened: and their faces were not ashamed.
6. This poor man cried, and the LORD heard him, and saved him out of all his troubles.
7. The angel of the LORD encampeth round about them that fear him, and delivereth them.
8. O taste and see that the LORD is good: blessed is the man that trusteth in him.
9. O fear the LORD, ye his saints: for there is no want to them that fear him.
10. The young lions do lack, and suffer hunger: but they that seek the LORD shall not want any good thing.

II Timothy 1:7:

For God hath not given us the spirit of fear; but of power, and of love, and of a sound mind.

Romans 8:15:

For ye have not received the spirit of bondage again to fear; but ye have received the Spirit of adoption, whereby we cry, Abba, Father.

I John 4:18:

There is no fear in love; but perfect love casteth out fear: because fear hath torment. He that feareth is not made perfect in love.

Isaiah 41:10:

Fear thou not; for I am with thee: be not dismayed; for I am thy God: I will strengthen thee; yea, I will help thee; yea, I will uphold thee with the right hand of my righteousness.

Deuteronomy 31:6:
Be strong and of a good courage, fear not, nor be afraid of them: for the Lord thy God, he it is that doth go with thee; he will not fail thee, nor forsake thee.

Mark 5:36:
Be not afraid, only believe.

Psalm 23:4:
Yea, though I walk through the valley of the shadow of death, I will fear no evil: for thou art with me; thy rod and thy staff they comfort me.

Matthew 10:29-31:
Verses:

29. Are not two sparrows sold for a farthing? and one of them shall not fall on the ground without your Father.
30. But the very hairs of your head are all numbered.
31. Fear ye not therefore, ye are of more value than many sparrows.

Pray the Word . . .

For Unsaved Children and Loved Ones

Luke 9:56:

For the Son of man is not come to destroy men's lives, but to save them.

Lord, since You have come to save, and since there is joy in heaven as stated in Luke 15:7, please, save my loved one!

Luke 15:7:

I say unto you, that likewise joy shall be in heaven over one sinner that repenteth, more than over ninety and nine just persons, which need no repentence.

II Peter 3:9:

The Lord is not slack concerning his promise, as some men count slackness; but is longsuffering to us-ward; not willing that any should perish, but that all should come to repentance.

LORD, IT IS NOT YOUR WILL THAT MY SON, DAUGHTER, OR LOVED ONE WOULD BE LOST, THEREFORE WE PRAY:

I John 5:14-15:

Verses:

14. And this is the confidence that we have in him, that, if we ask any thing according to his will, he heareth us:
15. And if we know that he hear us, whatsoever we ask, we know that we have the petitions that we desired of him.

Lord, You know that I John 5:14 & 15 says that we could have anything we asked if it is Your will. I know that Your will is that none should perish, so I know that this is the will of God for them to be saved, and Your Word says that You cannot lie.

Numbers 23:19:
God is not a man, that he should lie; neither the son of man, that he should repent: hath he said, and shall he not do it? Or hath he spoken, and shall he not make it good?

I'm believing for my child to be saved. I reach into the greedy jaws of hell and pull them out of the fire in Jesus' name! I resist Satan away from them. Put hunger in their hearts to serve You.

Jude 22-23:
Verses:
22. And of some have compassion, making a difference:
23. And others save with fear, pulling them out of the fire; hating even the garment spotted by the flesh.

Isaiah 54:13:
And all thy children shall be taught of the LORD; and great shall be the peace of thy children.

I pray Jacob's prayer:
Genesis 32:26:
I will not let thee go, except thou bless me.

I will not let go until my children and family are saved!

Jeremiah 31:33:

I will put my law in their inward parts, and write it in their hearts; and will be their God, and they shall be my people.

O God, put Your law and Your Spirit inside my children's hearts; be their God so they can be belong solely to You!

Pray the Word . . .

For Personal Growth

Psalm 138:8:

The LORD will perfect that which concerneth me: thy mercy, O LORD, endureth for ever: forsake not the works of thine own hands.

Psalm 139:1-4:

Verses:

1. O LORD, thou hast searched me, and known me.
2. Thou knowest my downsitting and mine uprising, thou understandest my thought afar off.
3. Thou compassest my path and my lying down, and art acquainted with all my ways.
4. For there is not a word in my tongue, but, lo, O LORD, thou knowest it altogether.

Psalm 19:13-14:

Verses:

13. Keep back thy servant also from presumptuous sins; let them not have dominion over me: then shall I be upright, and I shall be innocent from the great transgression.
14. Let the words of my mouth, and the meditation of my heart, be acceptable in thy sight, O LORD, my strength, and my redeemer.

Psalm 121:1-3:

Verses:

1. I will lift up mine eyes unto the hills, from whence cometh my help.
2. My help cometh from the LORD, which made heaven and earth.
3. He will not suffer my foot to be moved: he that keepeth me will not slumber.

Psalm 18:32-33:

Verses:

32. It is God that girdeth me with strength, and maketh my way perfect.
33. He maketh my feet like hinds' feet, and setteth me upon my high places.

Psalm 118:13-14:

Verses:

13. Thou hast thrust sore at me that I might fall: but the LORD helped me.
14. The LORD is my strength and song, and is become my salvation.

Psalm 51:10-12:

Verses:

10. Create in me a clean heart, O God; and renew a right spirit within me.
11. Cast me not away from thy presence; and take not thy holy spirit from me.
12. Restore unto me the joy of thy salvation; and uphold me with thy free spirit.

Matthew 6:9-13:

Verses:

9. After this manner therefore pray ye: Our Father which art in heaven, Hallowed be thy name.
10. Thy kingdom come. Thy will be done in earth, as it is in heaven.
11. Give us this day our daily bread.
12. And forgive us our debts, as we forgive our debtors.
13. And lead us not into temptation, but deliver us

from evil: For thine is the kingdom, and the power, and the glory, for ever. Amen.

Ephesians 1:17-18:

Verses:

17. That the God of our Lord Jesus Christ, the Father of glory, give unto me, the spirit of wisdom and revelation in the knowledge of him.
18. That the eyes of my understanding be enlightened; that I may know what is the hope of his calling, and what the riches of the glory of his inheritance in the saints.

Ephesians 3:16-19:

Verses:

16. That You would grant me, according to the riches of Your glory, to be strengthened with might by Your Spirit in the inner man;
17. That Christ may dwell in my heart by faith; so that I can be rooted and grounded in love,
18. That I may be able to comprehend with all saints what is the breadth, and length, and depth, and height:
19. And to know the love of Christ, which passeth knowledge, that I might be filled with all the fulness of God.

Lord, help me to add these things to my life:

II Peter 1:5-10:

Verses:

5. And beside this, giving all diligence, add to your **faith virtue**; and to virtue **knowledge**;
6. And to knowledge **temperance**; and to temper-

ance **patience**; and to patience **godliness**;

7. And to godliness **brotherly kindness**; and to brotherly kindness **charity**.
8. For if these things be in you, and abound, they make you that ye shall neither be barren nor unfruitful in the knowledge of our Lord Jesus Christ.
9. But he that lacketh these things is blind, and cannot see afar off, and hath forgotten that he was purged from his old sins.
10. Wherefore the rather, brethren, give diligence to make your calling and election sure: for if ye do these things, **ye shall never fall**.

O God, help me to never fall, but to abound and be a partaker of the divine nature adding to my faith the following:

Virtue
Knowledge
Temperance
Patience
Godliness
Brotherly Kindness
Charity

Pray the Word . . .

For Financial Blessings

Psalm 112:1-10:

Verses:

1. Praise ye the LORD. Blessed is the man that feareth the LORD, that delighteth greatly in his commandments.
2. His seed shall be mighty upon earth: the generation of the upright shall be blessed.
3. Wealth and riches shall be in his house: and his righteousness endureth for ever.
4. Unto the upright there ariseth light in the darkness: he is gracious, and full of compassion, and righteous.
5. A good man sheweth favour, and lendeth: he will guide his affairs with discretion.
6. Surely he shall not be moved for ever: the righteous shall be in everlasting remembrance.
7. He shall not be afraid of evil tidings: his heart is fixed, trusting in the LORD.
8. His heart is established, he shall not be afraid, until he see his desire upon his enemies.
9. He hath dispersed, he hath given to the poor; his righteousness endureth for ever; his horn shall be exalted with honour.
10. The wicked shall see it, and be grieved; he shall gnash with his teeth, and melt away: the desire of the wicked shall perish.

Isaiah 48:17:

I am the LORD thy God which teacheth thee to profit, which leadeth thee by the way that thou shouldest go.

Deuteronomy 8:18:

But thou shalt remember the LORD thy God: for it is he that giveth thee power to get wealth.

Teach us, Lord, to be good stewards and to get wealth so we can give more to Your kingdom, and our family can be blessed and all needs provided for sufficiently.

Malachi 3:10-11:

10. Bring ye all the tithes into the storehouse, that there may be meat in mine house, and prove me now herewith, saith the LORD of hosts, if I will not open you the windows of heaven, and pour you out a blessing, that there shall not be room enough to receive it.
11. And I will rebuke the devourer for your sakes, and he shall not destroy the fruits of your ground; neither shall your vine cast her fruit before the time in the field, saith the LORD of hosts.

Pray the Word . . .

Over the Great Commission

Luke 10:2:

Therefore said he unto them, The harvest truly is great, but the labourers are few: pray ye therefore the Lord of the harvest, that he would send forth labourers into his harvest.

Lord, may we go forth as laborers doing what we can do to proclaim the gospel of Jesus Christ!

Matthew 9:37-38:

Verses:

37. The harvest truly is plenteous, but the labourers are few;
38. Pray ye therefore the Lord of the harvest, that he will send forth labourers into his harvest.

Lord, we pray that the church will do what You told us to do in,

Mark 16:15:

And he said unto them, Go ye into all the world, and preach the gospel to every creature.

And Lord, go with us as you went with the early church, stated in,

Mark 16:20:

And they went forth, and preached every where, the Lord working with them, and confirming the word with signs following.

Lord, help us to obey Luke 14, and fill your house, and not excuse ourselves from doing the great commission!

Luke 14:16-23:

Verses:

16. Then said he unto him, A certain man made a great supper, and bade many:
17. And sent his servant at supper time to say to them that were bidden, Come; for all things are now ready.
18. And they all with one consent began to make excuse. The first said unto him, I have bought a piece of ground, and I must needs go and see it: I pray thee have me excused.
19. And another said, I have bought five yoke of oxen, and I go to prove them: I pray thee have me excused.
20. And another said, I have married a wife, and therefore I cannot come.
21. So that servant came, and shewed his lord these things. Then the master of the house being angry said to his servant, Go out quickly into the streets and lanes of the city, and bring in hither the poor, and the maimed, and the half, and the blind.
22. And the servant said, Lord, it is done as thou hast commanded, and yet there is room.
23. And the lord said unto the servant, Go out into the highways and hedges, and compel them to come in, that my house may be filled.

Pray the Word . . .

In Praise

Psalm 96:7-9:

Verses:

7. Give unto the Lord, O ye kindreds of the people, give unto the Lord glory and strength.
8. Give unto the Lord the glory due unto his name: bring an offering, and come into his courts.
9. O worship the Lord in the beauty of holiness: fear before him all the earth.

Psalm 99:1-3 & 5:

Verses:

1. The Lord reigneth; let the people tremble: he sitteth between the cherubims; let the earth be moved.
2. The Lord is great in Zion; and he is high above all the people.
3. Let them praise thy great and terrible name; for it is holy.
5. Exalt ye the Lord our God, and worship at his footstool; for he is holy.

Psalm 34:1-3:

Verses:

1. I will bless the Lord at all times: his praise shall continually be in my mouth.
2. My soul shall make her boast in the Lord: the humble shall hear thereof, and be glad.
3. O magnify the Lord with me, and let us exalt his name together.

Psalm 35:10:

All my bones shall say, Lord, who is like unto thee, which deliverest the poor from him that is too strong for him, yea, the poor and the needy from him that spoileth him?

Psalm 36:7-9:

Verses:

7. How excellent is thy lovingkindness, O God! Therefore the children of men put their trust under the shadow of thy wings.
8. They shall be abundantly satisfied with the fatness of thy house; and thou shalt make them drink of the river of thy pleasures.
9. For with thee is the fountain of life: in thy light shall we see light.

Revelation 19:1:

Alleluia; Salvation, and glory, and honour, and power, unto the Lord our God.

Revelation 4:11:

Thou art worthy, O Lord, to receive glory and honour and power: for thou hast created all things, and for thy pleasure they are and were created.

Revelation 5:12-13:

Verses:

12. Worthy is the Lamb that was slain to receive power, and riches, and wisdom, and strength, and honour, and glory, and blessing.
13. And every creature which is in heaven, and on the earth, and under the earth, and such as are in the sea, and all that are in them, heard I saying, Blessing, and honour, and glory, and power, be unto him that sitteth upon the throne, and

unto the Lamb for ever and ever.

Psalm 56:10:
In God will I praise his word: in the LORD will I praise his word.